THE
SKETCHBOOK
OF
VILLARD de
HONNECOURT

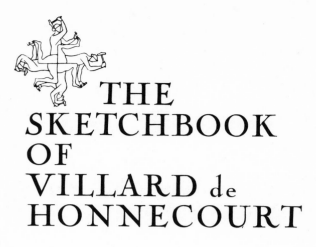

THE
SKETCHBOOK
OF
VILLARD de
HONNECOURT

Edited by THEODORE BOWIE

INDIANA UNIVERSITY PRESS
Bloomington and London

INTRODUCTION

Villard de honnecourt's *Sketchbook* is very well
known to students of medieval art. It has been the subject of
extensive research and commentary in the last hundred years,
and at least three facsimile editions of it have been published
within that period. The general student and the layman, however, have rarely seen more than a dozen plates of this *Sketchbook* in reproduction, out of a total of sixty-five. Most American
libraries do not seem to possess those editions; the latest and most
important of the studies, Hahnloser's *Kritische Gesamtausgabe*,
appears to be a bibliographical rarity. (The English translation
of this study had not appeared when the present edition was
being prepared.) The present edition, neither critical nor scholarly, of Villard's drawings, is intended for the nonspecialist. Its
indebtedness to Hahnloser as well as to his predecessors, Omont,
Willis, Lassus, Quicherat, and others, and to such modern com-
mentators as Panofsky, Focillon, and Branner, is explicit. The
Old French captions have been freshly translated by the Editor,
but where technical points of architecture or masonry are con-
cerned, the renderings are based on a consensus of authorities.
One major liberty has been taken. The order of the drawings
in the portfolio as it exists today is not necessarily the original
one. Many sheets have disappeared forever, and various owners
appear to have transposed the order of the folios. It therefore
seems useful to present the drawings according to the logic of
their subject matter, for the sake of the gain provided by juxta-
posing closely interrelated items. This could not be done with

absolute consistency because Villard was apt to sketch a drawing on any theme on the first available blank space. Professor Erwin Panofsky, among other scholars, warmly encouraged this idea and made a number of suggestions which were followed by the Editor in the second printing and incorporated here. (A Table of Concordance has been made for the benefit of those who might wish to compare the new order with the official one.)

Who precisely was Villard de Honnecourt? The curious thing is that we know nothing whatever about him that he has not told us, directly or inferentially, in this very *Sketchbook*. Honnecourt, which gave him his name, is a tiny village south of Cambrai which suffered much during both World Wars, and is today totally ignored by the *Guide Michelin*. It has no claim to fame other than this connection with an architect, or *maître d'oeuvre* (or *maître de chantier*), who evidently worked for the Cistercian Order, and who observed and studied the construction of such great churches as those of Cambrai, Rheims, Laon, and others. The information he gives us about these structures leads us to suppose that he was active between 1225 and 1250. Whether he himself was in charge of building the churches of Cambrai, Saint-Quentin, or some other town, we shall probably never know. He must have had a solid reputation to have been invited to Hungary where, as he tells us, he "remained for a long time." What he accomplished there is also a matter of surmise, as are the actual period of his journey and the connection which the *Sketchbook* may have had with it.

This *Sketchbook*, or *Album* as the French call it, constitutes MS. 19093 of the French Collection in the Bibliothèque Nationale in Paris. Prior to the Revolution it had been item No. 1104 in the Library of Saint-Germain-des-Prés, a gift some time in the seventeenth century from a member of the celebrated Félibien family. The book had apparently been a family heirloom since the late fifteenth century; the then owner made out that Villard belonged to his lineage, and in 1482 or 1483 he or one of his descendants added an inscription, now faintly visible, in the slab of the *Incipit* (plate 1) to the effect that "my ancestor, Alexis de Félibien, sire de Montgognie," had designed the "engines" to be found in this book. This Alexis de Félibien would thus presumably have been a pupil or follower of Villard, and the *Sketchbook* would have been his by direct transmittal.

There is no doubt that several hands other than Villard's have contributed some drawings (with appropriate captions), particularly in the section devoted to the application of practical geometry to problems of masonry and carpentry. As it stands, the *Sketchbook* consists of thirty-three parchment folios folded once and bound in pigskin. Their average dimensions are 160 mm. by 240 mm. (roughly 6¼ inches by 10½ inches). The book is a palimpsest in parts. On some pages, the design on the verso is perceptible; on others, there is a rubbing off or a stamping of the drawing on the page opposite. Villard's practice seems to have been to make a sketch in the equivalent of lead or silver point, and then to trace a firm outline in ink. Scholarly opinion inclines toward the theory that, in his figures, where the outline is left bare, he is copying sculpture, and that where there is shading, he is trying to suggest the values of painting. His captions are always in a highly legible script, contrary to that of some later contributors. He seems to have used some kind of sepia or bistre ink with which he produced effects of great subtlety, especially in his shadings, so that his original line appears to the modern eye to be much less harsh than black-and-white photography would lead one to suppose.

The drawings pose a number of unresolved questions. What was Villard's purpose in making them? Was he compiling a work guide for his shop, and an aide-mémoire for his own needs? Did he prepare this guide with the Hungarian trip in mind? How many drawings are the result of direct observation, how many are copies and adaptations, how many were made from memory, and, if so, how long after the experience? Such questions are meat and drink to art historians, who have not failed to point to this and that source, this affinity, and that echo. The evidence before our eyes convinces us that while the greater number of the drawings were done at the height of Villard's activity, he certainly must have revised the *Sketchbook* late in life, altering designs and adding remarks and therefore conferring on it the benefit of retrospection. What stands out after more than six centuries is the freshness of Villard's approach to his task. He is not perhaps a first-rate draughtsman; he is rather innocent of perspective; his elevations proceed by stages rather than as total concepts; his iconography is sometimes shaky, and his technical vocabulary limited. But what intellectual curiosity, what independence of judgment, what an eye for the structurally sound, the artistically valid, and the useful! He knows and respects ancient sculpture, just as he admires the architecture of Rheims Cathedral. He is curious about lion-taming, and is anxious for us to know that the big lion was drawn from life. What to us may be a trivial gadget, like the Tantalus cup, stirs his fancy, and like many a more celebrated figure, he tinkers with a perpetual motion machine. He is always on the lookout for simple and practical methods of work, such as his idea for drawing human and animal figures based on simple geometric forms. His tone is informal but authoritative; he is thoroughly French in his direct simplicity, in his tastes, and in his occasional lack of reverence: "The Bishop's hands will never get cold," says he with a reference to a brass hand warmer he is describing; let him boldly use it "at High Mass," provided, he implies, he doesn't spill the coals. The mood of skepticism is missing, however. No man was ever more of his own time, as Focillon remarks in *L'Art d'Occident*. Here is as true, unadorned, unaffected, and enthusiastic a witness of High Gothic as we could wish, and we yield to the delight of poring over a technical handbook which is also a personal document of psychological as well as artistic interest.

The present edition, formally prepared as a publication of Indiana University Press, is actually the successor of two private printings made possible (in 1959 and 1961) by grants from the Research Committee of Indiana University.

BIBLIOGRAPHY

FACSIMILE AND CRITICAL EDITIONS

Facsimile of the Sketch-book of Wilars de Honecort ... published
by M. Alfred Darcel from the MS. of M. J. B. A. Lassus ...
translated, edited, and augmented ... by the Rev. Robert
Willis. London, John Henry and James Parker, 1859.

Album de Villard de Honnecourt, architecte du XIIIe Siècle.
(Published for the Département des Manuscrits of the Bib-
liothèque Nationale by Henri Omont.) Paris, Berthaud
Frères, 1906. (Later editions: 1926, 1931.)

*Villard de Honnecourt—Kritische Gesamtausgabe des Bauhütten-
buches, ms. fr. 19093 der Pariser Nationalbibliotek.* Richard
Hahnloser, Wien, A. Schroll, 1935.

ARTICLES

Robert Branner, "Three Problems from the Villard de Honnecourt Manuscript." *Art Bulletin*, XXIX, No. 1, pp. 61-66
(March 1957).

———, "A Note on Gothic Architects and Scholars." *The Bur-
lington Magazine*, XCIX, No. 656, pp. 372-73 (Nov. 1957).

Charles Rufus Morey, "Villard de Honnecourt—Kritische Gesamtausgabe ..." *Art Bulletin*, XVII, No. 4, pp. 509-11 (De-
cember 1935).

Erwin Panofsky, "The History of the Theory of Human Propor-
tions as a Reflection of the History of Styles," now consti-
tuting Chapter 2 of his *Meaning in the Visual Arts*. New
York, Doubleday Anchor Books, 1955.

10

THE
PLATES
AND THEIR
DESCRIPTIONS

THE descriptions follow the general pattern of the pages, starting at the top and reading from left to right, except when a drawing is placed in a reverse direction. In this edition some of the pages have been inverted or half-inverted; these changes in the original position are always clearly indicated.

As has been noted, the sequence of the plates has been altered to conform to the inner logic of the subjects. To simplify the search for the concordance, the indication C. and a roman numeral, which refers to the standard order, are used. The information is repeated in a Table of Concordance at the back of the book.

The last page of the *Sketchbook* is entirely devoted to two recipes: one for a pick-me-up to relieve the effects of any accident, such as a fall, incurred in the course of erecting a building, and the other, for a method to retain the fresh colors of flowers used to prepare painting materials. This page is neither reproduced nor translated here.

Translations of the inscriptions are in italics.

PLATE 1   INCIPIT   (C.I)

The indications *N. 1104 and S.G. lat 1104* and *St. Germani a Pratis* inform us that the Album was once in the Library of Saint-Germain-des-Prés. The stamp of the Bibliothèque Nationale goes back to the period of the Revolution.

Top row: A pelican, standing on a globe, and tearing at its breast; a mitred bishop, seated and holding a crozier; a night owl.

Bottom row: A magpie holding a cross in its beak, standing on a slab (see Introduction for a comment on the inscription) at the right side of which crouches a goat-like demon.

S. Germani a Pratis

N. 1104.

PLATE 2   THE TWELVE APOSTLES
            AND OTHER FIGURES   (c.ii)

*Here you will find the images of the Twelve Apostles, sitting.
Villard de Honnecourt greets you and begs all who will use the
devices found in this book to pray for his soul and remember
him. For in this book will be found sound advice on the virtues
of masonry and the uses of carpentry. You will also find strong
help in drawing figures according to the lessons taught by the art
of geometry.*

The Apostles are seated in three rows, two at the top and five
in each of the lower rows. The other figures, standing on the top
row, are a monk and a hooded woman. The somersaulting woman
is presumed to represent Salome.

Ci poeis uos trouer les ágres des .XIII. apostles
en seant .

ſ Vilars dehonecort il salue ⁊ ſi proie a tos ceus qui de ces engiens
ouuerront · con trouera en cest liure qʼl proient por ſarme
⁊ quil lor souuengne delui · Car en cest liure puet õ trouer grant
consel de le grant force demaconerie ⁊ des engiens de carpenterie ·
⁊ ſi trouerés le force dele por   traiture · les trais ensi come li ars
de iometrie le commãd   ⁊ ensaigne ·

PLATE 3   CHRIST IN MAJESTY   (C.XXXII)

PLATE 4   CHRIST IN MAJESTY   (C.XXI)

Below the seated figure of Christ is an ornamental volute (similar to those in Plates 53 and 54) topped by a dragon.

PLATE 5   THE CHURCH TRIUMPHANT   (C.VIII)

PLATE 6   TWO STANDING MEN   (C.LV)

The figure on the right is a Prophet, that on the left an Apostle.

(Plate inverted from the original position)

PLATE 7 THE FLAGELLATION OF CHRIST
(C.LVI)

The actual flagellation takes place at the top. At the bottom, Christ is returned to Pilate.

PLATE 8   DESCENT FROM THE CROSS   (C.XXVI)

Three men are taking Christ down. The Virgin stands on the left and Saint John the Baptist on the right, while Joseph of Arimathea collects the Blood.

On the inverse side of the sheet, the Lion of St. Mark and the Bull of St. Luke hover.

(Plate inverted from the original position)

PLATE 9   CHRIST ON THE CROSS   (C.IV)

The crude skull at the base of the cross is by a later hand.

PLATE 10   MONUMENTAL CRUCIFIX
AND TWO PENDANTS   (C.XV)

In this design, the Virgin and St. John, each identified by abbreviated inscriptions, stand on volutes on either side of the Crucified One. Professor Panofsky suggests that the word "HEL" inscribed above the Christ is a form of "EL," "the first name of God." He also points out that the pendant on the right, obviously by a different and later hand, offers an instructive example of the change that took place between the Early Gothic phase represented by Villard and the terminal phase starting about 1300. The specific proof is the transformation of the "C" curve of the body of Christ on the crucifix into a zigzag in the pendant.

PLATE 11 FIGURE OF PLEADING WOMAN
(c.xxiii)

The inscription on the right reads: *This is one of the two women who stood judgment before Solomon because of the child that each one claimed as her own.*

Ceſci lune deſ · 15 · damoizieles
de q̇ li iugemenſ fu faiſ devāt
ſalemon de leur enfant. ɠ̇aſſeu
ne uoloit auoir

PLATE 12   THREE FIGURES OF MEN   (C.XXIV)

Top row: Seated lord and standing bishop.

Bottom row: One of the Magi pointing to the Star of the Nativity.

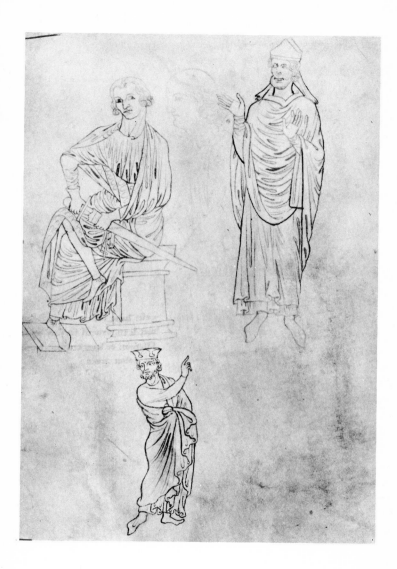

PLATE 13   TWO ALLEGORICAL FIGURES
            (C.VI)

Left: A horseman thown from his mount. The inscription above him reads: *How Pride stumbleth.*

Right: Seated figure of a woman holding a globe on which is designed a dove. The inscription defines her as *Humility*.

PLATE 14   SEATED KING   (C.XLIX)

PLATE 15   SEVEN FIGURES   (C.XXV)

The inscription at the right top, reads: *This is a king and these are his soldiers and his retinue.*

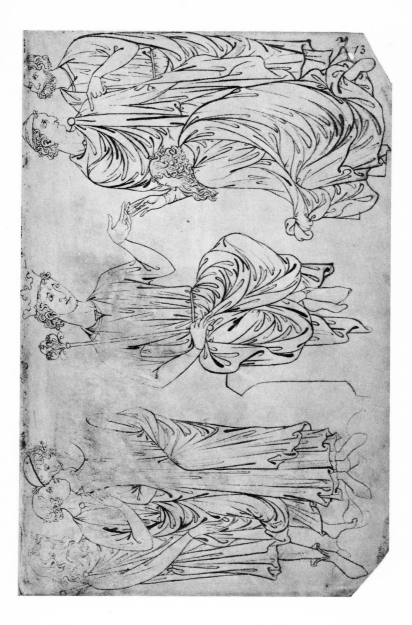

PLATE 16 TWO SEATED FIGURES (C.XXVII)

A lord and a lady seated side by side; the lord holds a falcon on his gloved right hand.

Above the schematic plan of the apse and crossing of a church, the inscription reads: *Here is the presbytery* [chancel?] *of the Church of Our Lady of Vauxcelles, a church of the Cistercian Order.*

Below, above a crouching figure, the inscription reads: *This is a picture of Our Lord as He stumbled.*

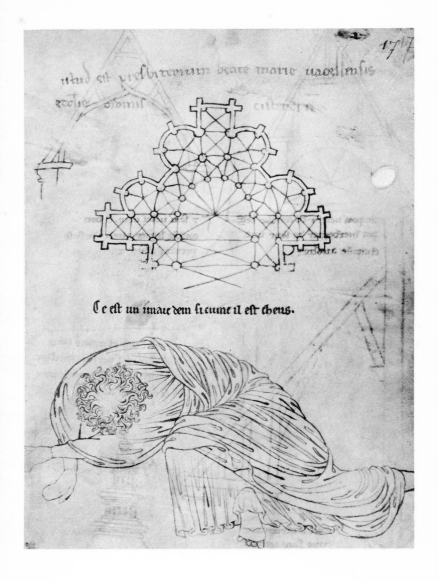

istud est presbiterium beate marie uaceliensis

Ce est un imaie dem si cume il est cheus.

PLATE 18   TWO UNRELATED SKETCHES
(C.XLVI)

Left: Figure of a half-crouching man (note the similarity with the Stumbling Christ in the preceding plate).

Right: Knight with one foot in stirrup, about to mount his horse.

(Plate half-inverted from the original position)

PLATE 19   TWO KNIGHTS ON HORSEBACK
(C.XVI)

The riders face one another as if about to joust. The tree drawn
in the center of the shield carried by the rider on the right is by a
later hand.

PLATE 20 TWO UNRELATED SKETCHES
(C.III)

To the left: a four-antennaed snail coming out of its shell.

To the right: a standing warrior wearing chain armor and helmet. The inscription to the left (in 15th-century script) reads: *De Honnecourt, he who went to Hungary*.

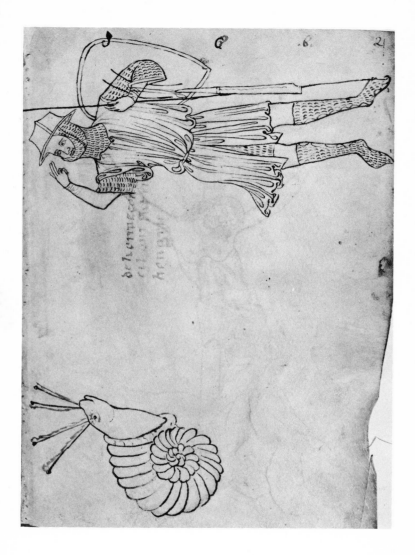

Christ is holding an orb. The archer and the soldier wielding a lance do not seem to be related to the divine figure.

(Plate half-inverted from the original position)

PLATE 22   BIRDS, DOGS, AND HUMANS   (C.LI)

At the top: two parrots, perched.

At the bottom: a minstrel playing a viol to a dancing dog, woman with parrot and dog.

PLATE 23   NUDE MALE   (C.XXII)

Holding a vase of flowers, the nude male stands beside an altar above which there is the image of a crowned, seated king. In the entire *Sketchbook* there is no other nude figure with bistre shading.

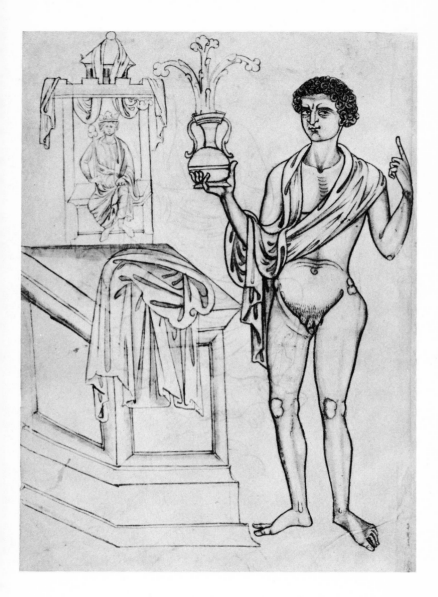

PLATE 24 WALKING MAN (C.LVIII)

The man is wearing a chlamys and skullcap.

PLATE 25 TWO MALE NUDES AND
DECORATIVE HEADS (C.XLIII)

The seated man wears a Phrygian cap, while the standing nude, with a chlamys around his shoulders, holds a staff. The two foliate heads are simpler than those reproduced in Plate 26.

PLATE 26   FOLIATE ORNAMENTS   (C.X)

At the top: two foliate heads of bearded men.

In the center: an ornamental band.

At the bottom: ornamental leaves.

PLATE 27   "SARACEN'S TOMB"   (C.XI)

The inscription at the top reads: *I once saw the sepulchre of a Saracen which looked like this.* "Saracen" is taken to mean any pagan, including a Roman.

PLATE 28 MISCELLANEOUS DESIGNS
AND INSTRUCTIONS (C.XVII)

At the bottom of the page, a pair of men playing at dice or checkers. Above them, a boar and a hare, out of scale with one another. When the plate is inverted, the designs are related to the copious text. The figure with concentric circles on the left is a hand warmer, seen in plan, while on the right is a Tantalus cup. The inscriptions read as follows:

If you wish to make a hand warmer, you must first make a kind of brass apple with two fitting halves. Inside this brass apple, there must be six brass rings, each with two pivots, and in the middle there must be a little brazier with two pivots. The pivots must be alternated in such a way that the brazier always remains upright, for each ring bears the pivots of the others. If you follow the instructions and the drawing, the coals will never drop out, no matter which way the brazier is turned. A bishop may freely use this device at High Mass; his hands will not get cold as long as the fire lasts. That is all there is to it.

Here is a siphon which may be made in a cup in such a way that there is a little tower in its middle, and in the middle of that a tube reaching down to the bottom of the cup. The tube must be as long as the cup is deep. And in the tower there must be three cross-channels against the bottom of the cup so that the wine in the cup may go into the tube. Above the tower, there should be a bird with its beak held so low that it may drink when the cup is full. The wine will then flow through the tube and the foot of the cup, which is double. The bird should obviously be hollow too.

(Plate inverted from the original position)

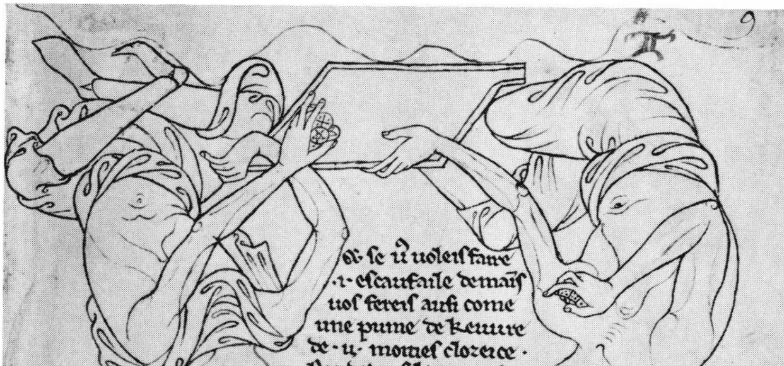

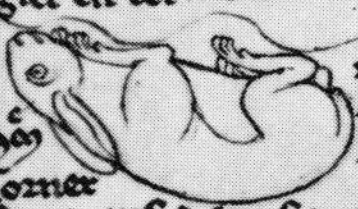

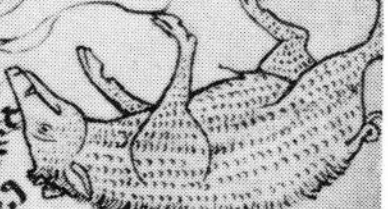

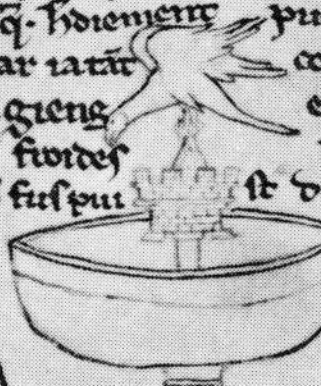

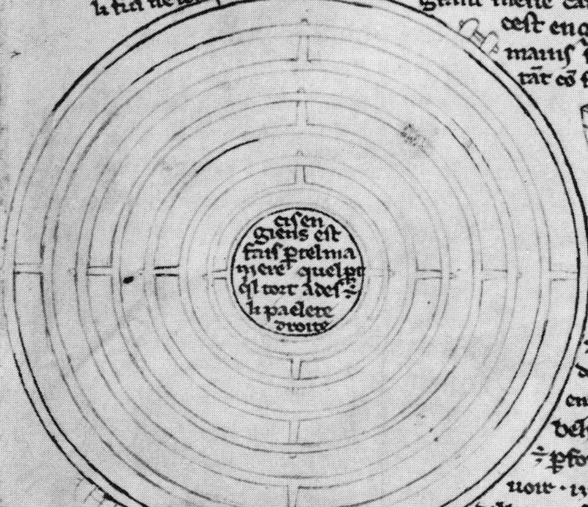

PLATE 30   SCENES OF VIOLENCE   (C.LIII)

To the right: the inscription identifies the two saints being de-
capitated as Cosmas and Damian.

To the left: a gladiator holding a lion at bay with a pike.

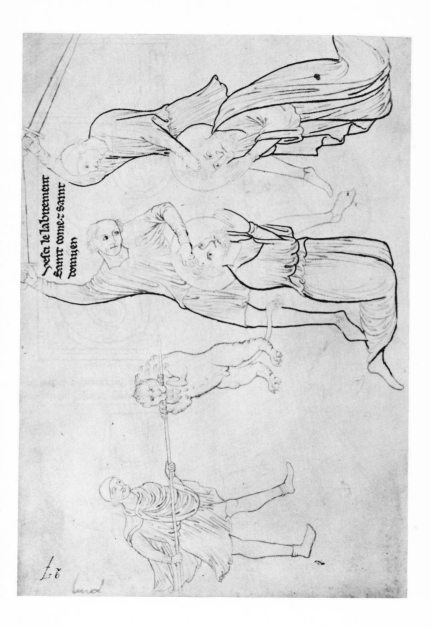

PLATE 31   LION TRAINER AND LION   (C.XLVII)

A lion trainer with two dogs faces Leo, chained. To the right is the head of another lion.

The inscription reads: *I want to describe how a lion is trained. The lion's trainer has two dogs. Whenever he wishes the lion to obey his command, and the lion growls, he beats his dogs. This puzzles the lion so much that, when he sees the dogs beaten, his own spirits are dampened, and he does what is ordered. If he is angry, there is no use trying, for he will do nothing either with good or bad treatment. Please note that this lion was drawn from life.*

(Plate inverted from the original position)

Be len fangnement del
lion iu uel ge pleir
eil q le lio doctrine
il a ·ii· chaaus
qant il uelt lehon
faire faire aucune core se li
comande · se li lions groigne
il bat ses chaaus · dont a lilions grãt
doutance qant il uoit les kaiaus
batre · se refraint sõ corage · z fait
co cõ li comand · z fil est coreciés secco
ne peruoil me · car il ne feroit por
ne lun ne tort ne droit · z bien sachés
q cel lions fu contrefais il uist.

PLATE 32   LION AND PORCUPINE   (c.xlviii)

The inscription under LEO reads: *Here is a lion seen from the front. Please remember that he was drawn from life.*

The inscription above the porcupine reads: *This is a porcupine, a little beast that shoots its quills when aroused.*

Leco

vesa ı. lion ſi cort
on le voit pʒ deuant
ʒ ſaues bien qʒl fu
contrefais al uıſ.

vesci ı. poʒc eſpı.
ceſt une bieſte lere
qı lance ſe ſoıe qant
ele ʒ coʒreıe.

PLATE 33   BEAR AND SWAN   (C.VII)

The castellated mansion at the bottom right is taken to represent the City of Heaven.

PLATE 34 MISCELLANEOUS ANIMAL FORMS
(C.XIV)

Grasshopper, cat, house fly, dragon-fly, crustacean, and coiled dog. To the right: a labyrinth in plan.

PLATE 35   DIAGRAMMATIC FIGURES I
(C.XXXV)

The inscriptions in French and Latin at the bottom right both say the same thing: *Here begins the method of representation.* "Portraiture," the word used, can mean portrayal, delineation, etc.

With the exception of the portrait of a bearded and tonsured monk at the upper left, the figures in this and the next three plates are based on geometrical forms: Virgin and child; stag; enthroned king; thrasher and two standing men.

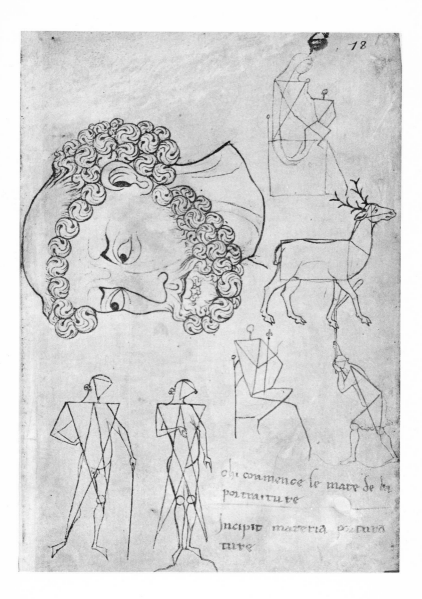

Chi commence le mate de la portraiture

Incipit materia pictura ture

PLATE 36 DIAGRAMMATIC FIGURES II
(C.XXXVI)

The inscription at the lower right reads: *Here begins the method of representation as taught by the art of geometry, to facilitate work. Elsewhere you will find the method of masonry.*

A castellated tower and wall; head of a horse; five human faces; greyhound; extended left hand; a grazing sheep; a spread eagle; two intersecting ostriches.

Ci comence li force des trais de portraiture si conli ars de iometrie lel enfaigne por legierement ouver. Fir en lautre fuiel se cil dle maconerie.

PLATE 37   DIAGRAMMATIC FIGURES III
(C.XXXVII)

Top row: Incomplete double figure; warrior; man with scythe; kneeling man.

Second row: two intersecting trumpeters; hooded falconer; man with arms akimbo.

Third row: two groups of wrestlers; mounted knight.

Bottom right: intersecting lionesses, seated; Virgin and Child, enthroned; two flowers.

PLATE 38   DIAGRAMMATIC FIGURES IV
(C.XXXVIII)

Top row: Four masons revolving in a broken cross, or "fylfot;" three fishes with one head.

Middle: helmeted head; quadrated face.

Bottom: Four workers seen in isometric elevation; head of wild boar in profile.

The inscription reads: *On these four pages are figures of the art of geometry, but to understand them one must be careful to learn the particular use of each.*

en cef · iiii · fuelles a deſfigures de
lart de iometrie · mais al conoiſtre
couient auoir gͬut eſgart lͥ ſauoir
uelt de ⁒ caſcune doit ourer

PLATE 39 PLAN OF THE TOWER OF LAON
CATHEDRAL (c.xviii)

Below the plan the inscription reads: *As you will learn from this book, I have been in many lands, but nowhere have I seen a tower like that of Laon. Here is the plan of the first story* [above the level of the façade] *with the first windows. At this level, the tower has eight sides. The turrets are square, with their columns in groups of three. Then come small arches and entablatures and turrets with eight columns, and between two columns a bull. Then some more small arches and entablatures and eight-sided roofs. On each face there is a big arch to give light. By looking carefully at the drawings before you, you will perceive the whole arrangement and the elevation and the way the turrets change shape. Remember that if you wish to build great buttress towers, they must project sufficiently. Take pains with your work and you will act prudently and wisely.*

At the bottom of the page there is a tabernacle and the inverted head of a bearded man.

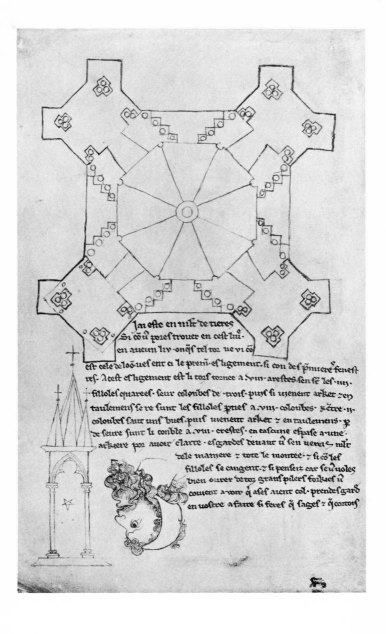

Ja este en nise de nieres
Si con poes trouer en cest lu
en aucun liu onqs tel tor ne vi con

est cele de looues ent ci le prem̄ es ligement. si con des pmiere fenes
res. a cest es ligement est li tors tornee a .viii. arestes sens sē les .viii.
filloles quarees. seur colonbes de trois puis si uienent arker zẽ
taulemens se re sunt les filloles pres a .vii. colonbes. z ẽtre .ii.
colonbes sant uns bues. puis uienent arker z en taulemens. p̄
de seure sunt li conble a .viii. crestes. en cascune espase a une
arkiere por auoir clarte. esgardes deuant u sen uenes. nīt
dele manyere z tote le montee. z si con les
filloles se cangent. z si penses car seu uoles
bien ouer de tos grans pilers forkies il
conient a uoir q̄ ases auert col. prendes gard
en uostre afaire si feres q̄ sages z q̄ cortois

PLATE 40 TOWER OF LAON CATHEDRAL
(C.XIX)

This is the North Tower, seen in elevation.

PLATE 41   UNRELATED FIGURES AND PLANS
(C.XXIII)

At the bottom: a wrestling pair.

Upper right: the inscription below this plan reads: *This is a square church designed for the Cistercian Order.*

Upper left: The inscription below this plan reads: *This is the plan of the apse and the choir* [chevet] *of our Lady of Cambrai as it is now rising from the ground. Elsewhere in this book you will see the inner and outer elevations, as well as the design of the chapels, the walls and the flying buttresses.*

(There are no other drawings of Cambrai in the *Sketchbook*.)

(Plate inverted from the original position)

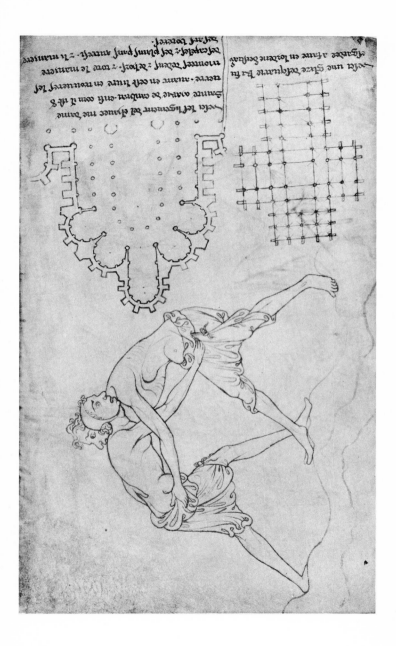

Vesci une glize desquarie ki fu
esgardee a faire en l'ordene de cistiaus

Vesci les figures des .iiii. evangelistes

Vesci le figement del clauier une dame
sainte marie de cambrai ensi com il est
deus · auant en est figure en ceu livre ki
monter devant le roi · z les · z tote le maniere
des estales · des plains pans atret · z la maniere
des arceteres z de l'ouraigne tot ensi com il est
fait et tornet.

PLATE 42   RHEIMS CATHEDRAL I   (C.LXI)

Exterior view of the circular apse. The inscription, placed at the left of the design on Plate 43, reads: [Here] *you may see the elevation of the chapels of the Church of Rheims from the out- side, just as they are from top to bottom. If those at Cambrai are done properly they will look like this. The upper entablature must have crenelations.*

PLATE 43   RHEIMS CATHEDRAL II   (C.LX)

31

Elevation of the apse, interior view. The inscription at the top reads: *Here is the elevation of the chapels of the Church of Rheims and how they are arranged on the inside. You may see the inner passages and the blind arches.*

(The inscriptions to the left pertain to the exterior view reproduced in Plate 42.)

Z en cele autre pagene poes u veir les montees des
capieles de le glire de rains par dehors tres le
comencement deca enle fin ensi com eles sont.
dautrerel maniere doiuent estre celes
de cambrai son lor fait droit. li
daerrains entaulemens doit
faire creniaus.

Vesci le
droite moitie
des capeles
de le glise
de rains 5
toute le man-
tere ensi com
eles sunt p-
deueris droite
enlor estage

Ves ci les voie
deuens 7 les
orbes arkes.

PLATE 44   RHEIMS CATHEDRAL III   (C.LXIII)

Top: Four architectonic details of the pillars. The inscription above the top row reads: *Here you may see one of the pillars of the Church of Rheims, one of those between two chapels, one on the lateral wall, and one from the nave of the edifice. The joints of all those pillars are as they should be.*

Center: Structural details. The two-line inscription below them reads: *Here are the molds of the chapels on the page opposite* [reproduced on Plate 45], *the tracery, the windows proper, the ogives, the transverse ribs, and the superarches above.*

The inscription at the bottom of the page pertains to Plate 45, and since it is terminated on the long side of that drawing, the full text of the translation adjoins that plate.

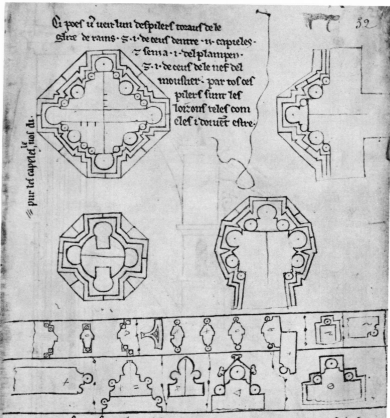

32

Ci poes vr veir ·iiii· despilers traus de le
glize de rains · S · i · de ceus dentre ·ii· capteles
z sema · i · del plampen
· S · i · de ceus de le nef del
mouster · par tos ces
pilers sunt les
loicons reles com
eles i donuet estre.

≡ pur les captel uos di

Veci le molle des chapteles de cele pagne la deuant · des formes z des
uerieres · des ogiues z des doublaus · z des sorvols ꝑ de seure ·

Veci les montees de leglize de rains z del plain pen · dedens z de hors ·
Li premiers estaulement des acantes doit faire cretaus si est puist
auoir uoie deuant le couertic · encontre ce couertic sunt les voies dedens ·
z ẽtant ces uoies sunt uolses z entaulees · dont reuienent les uoies de hors
ꝏ puet aler deuant les suels des uerieres · en lentaulement daertan doit auoir
cretaus ꝏ puist aler deuant le couertic · Ves aluec les manieres de uotes les
montrei.

PLATE 45   RHEIMS CATHEDRAL IV   (C.LXII)

Exterior and interior elevations of the lateral walls. The descrip-
tion statement, begun at the bottom of Plate 44 and continuing
on the side of this Plate, reads as follows:

*Here are the elevations of the Church of Rheims and the inner
and outer walls. The first entablatures of the side-aisles must be
crenelated so that there may be a passageway before the roof.
The inner galleries [triforia] are at the level of this roof. Above
these vaults and entablatures we find other passageways which
allow circulation in front of the window sills. The last entablature must have crenelations to permit passage before the roof.
Here is the model of all the elevations.*

*Consider well these elevations. Before the roof of the side-
aisles there must be a passageway over the entablature and there
must be another at the top in front of the windows, with low
crenelations, as you see in the picture before you. On the tops of
the pillars, there should be angels, and, in front, flying buttresses.
Before the great roof, there must also be passageways and crenelated tablements, to allow circulation in case of fire. And on the
tablement, there must be gutters to carry off the water. I say the
same for the chapels.*

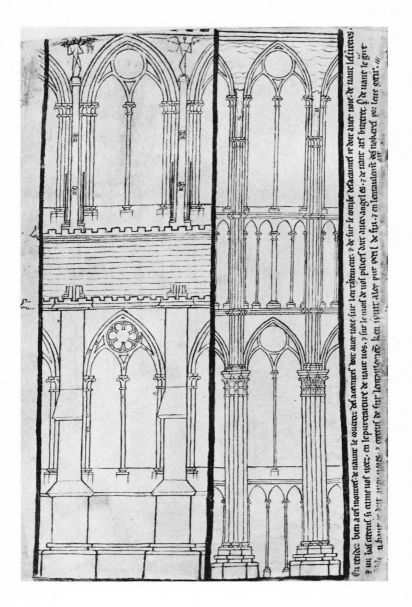

PLATE 46   RHEIMS CATHEDRAL V   (C.XX)

Detail of a window.

Below: The inscription on the left reads: *This is one of the windows of Rheims, in the area of the nave, as it stands between two pillars. I had been invited to go to Hungary when I drew this, which is why I liked it all the more.*

Above: The Virgin and Child.

veſci une deſ formeſ deraınſ
deſ eſpaſeſ dele neſ reteſ com
cleſ ſunt entre · ıı· pılerſ ·
Jeſtoıe mandeſ en le tıerre de
hongrıe qant ıo le portraıſ
p̃̃o lamaı ıo mıex ·

PLATE 47   RHEIMS CATHEDRAL VI   (C.LXIV)

Schematic view of the wall above the side aisle (with the trifo-rium omitted) and of the double row of flying buttresses.

Above: The inscription at the bottom of the page (and partly repeated in Latin inside the design by a later hand) reads: *This is a church with a double ambulatory designed by Villard de Honnecourt and Pierre de Corbie.*

Below: The second plan is labeled immediately below as follows: *This is the plan of the Church of St. Stephen at Meaux.* The Latin inscription in the design misleadingly calls it the Choir of St. Faron at Meaux.

15

Vesci les ligement de le glize de miax de saint esteune.
Desfaure est une glize a double charole. kpilars deshoneort trouat pie
ref de corhta.

PLATE 49   ARCHITECTURAL DETAILS   (c.xxx)

Top: to the left, a design labeled as follows: *Once when I was in Hungary, where I remained for a long time, I saw the paving of a church with this design.* To the right, plan of a column with the label above it reading: *Here is an example of how to build a pillar with the right joints.*

Below: A rose window, labeled as follows: *Here is the window of the Church of Our Lady of Chartres.* [West façade.]

108

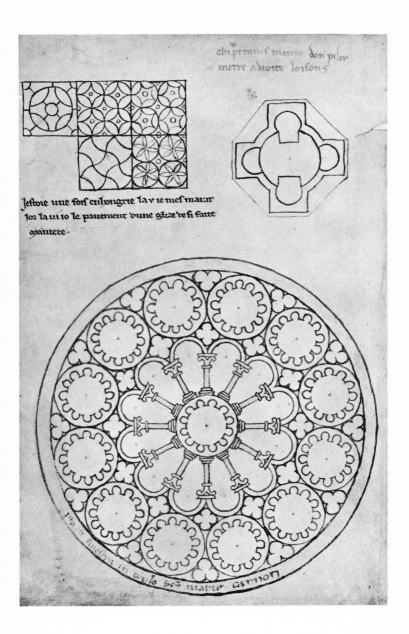

Jestoie une fois enhongrie la v te mes marir
Jo2 la iu io le pauement dune glize defi farte
oxaniere.

PLATE 50   A ROSE WINDOW   (C.XXI)

The inscription, in French and Latin, reads: *This is a round window in the Church of Lausanne.*

The drawing of a seated prophet at bottom left is unrelated.

16

Cest une reonde veriere dele glize delozane

hu et fenestra in losana ecclia

PLATE 51 A CLOCK TOWER (c.xii)

The inscription reads: *This is a clock tower. Whoever wishes to build a clock tower should study this one that I once saw. The first story is square, with four small gables. The second story has eight panels and a roof, and above that four smaller gables with a broad space between each. The topmost story is square, with four gables and an eight-sided roof. Here is a picture of it.*

Upper right: The initial S ornamented with a dragon is not related.

cest li maſons   ſon oʒoluge

Ki uelt faire le maſon dune
ierloge uel ent et une q̃ io
tu une fois. li pꝛimierz
eſtages de deſoſ eſt quareſ
a · iiij · puignonciauſ ·
li eſtages de ſerre eſt
a · viij · penſauſ · ꝫ puiſ
couertie · ꝫ puiſ · iiij ·
puignonciauſ · entre
· ij · puignonſ · i ·
eſpaſſe ſuit
li eſtages toſ de ſerre
ſeſt q̃res a · iiij · puig
nonciauſ · ꝫ li cōbleſ
a · viij · coſteſ · ſel
aluec le poꝛtrait ·

PLATE 52   DESIGN FOR A LECTERN   (c.xiii)

The inscription to the right reads: *Whoever wishes to build a lectern for the reading of the Gospel will learn that this is the best way to do it. First of all, place three dragons at the base, and a trefoiled slab over them. On top of that, three other dragons going in other directions, with columns as tall as the dragons topped by a triangular slab. The picture clearly shows how the lectern is made. In the middle of the columns there must be a stem to hold the pummel on which stands the eagle.*

Ki velt faire · i · letrif por suſ lire
evangille. veſ ent ci le mellor
maniere que io ſace · premiers a
p tierre · iiii · ſarpenſ · z puiſ une
aiſ a · iiii · compaſ de ſevre · z par
deſeure · iiii · ſarpenſ d'autre
maniere · z colonbeſ de
le hauture deſ ſarpenſ
z p deſeure · i · triangle
apreſ iu veſ bien de
confaite maniere li
letriſ eſt · veſ ent ci le
portrait · en mi liv deſ · iiii ·
colonbeſ doit avoir une
verge q̇ porte le
punnel ſor eoſ li
aile ſiet

PLATE 53 DESIGN FOR A CHOIR STALL
(C.LVII)

The inscription to the right reads: *If you wish to make a good poppet for a stall, copy this one.*

Se iu uoles bien ourer
Dune bone pourre a
uns estaus acesu ie rene

PLATE 54   TWO DESIGNS FOR CHOIR STALLS
(C.LIV)

The inscription under the design at left top reads: *Here is an easily built poppet for a stall with a partition and arm rest.*

The inverted image of a standing Christ or prophet is clearly related to the figures in Plates 3 and 4 above.

ſeſt une legiere poupee dunſ
eſtauſ a · i · entrecloſ atore le clef ·

PLATE 55   GEOMETRICAL DEVICES I
(MASONRY) (C.XXXIX)

Scholars are inclined to agree that the inscription in the little box at bottom right, which reads: *All these devices were extracted from geometry*, was inserted by a later hand. It implies that the drawings in Plates 55 to 57 and possibly even 58 through 60 were copied from a handbook of practical geometry.

The labels read from left to right, as follows:

Top row: How to measure the diameter of a column, only part of which is visible; How to find the midpoint of a drawn circle; How to cut the mold of a three-foot arch; How to arch a vault with an outer covering; How to make an apse with twelve windows; How to cut the springing-stone of an arch.

Second row: How to bring together two stones if they are not too far apart; How to cut a voussoir for a round building; How to cut an oblique voussoir.

Third row: How to make a bridge over water, with twenty-foot timbers; How to lay out a cloister with its galleries and courtyard; How to measure the width of a watercourse without crossing it; How to measure the width of a distant window.

Fourth row: How to place the four cornerstones of a cloister without plumb line or level; How to divide a stone so that each of its halves is square; How to shape the screw of a press; How to make two vessels so that one holds more than the other.

Bottom row: How to cut a regular voussoir.

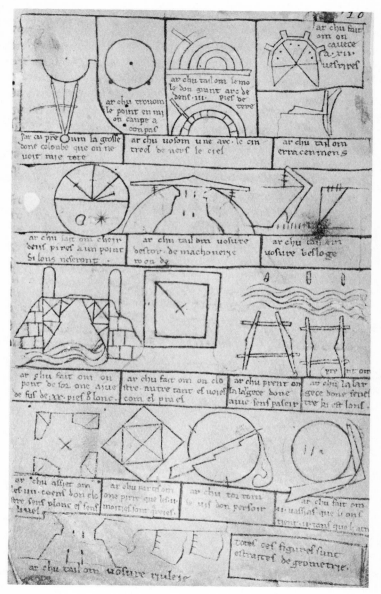

ar chu fait
om on
cauece
a .xii.
uesures

ar chu trouom
le point en mi
on caupe a
con pas

ar chu tail om le mo
le don guant arc de
dens .iii. pies de
tere

par cu pre̅ om la grosse
done colonbe que on ne
uoit mie tote

ar chu uos om une ave le cin
tres de nerf le ciel

ar chu tail om
erracentuens

ar chu fait om cheir
dens pires a un point
si lons neseront

ar chu tail om uosure
destor de machonerie
won de

ar chu tail om
uosure besloge

ar chu fait om on
pont de tor one ajue
de fust be .xx. pies s lone

ar chu fait om on clo
stre autre tant es uoies
com es pra es

ar chu pre̅t om
la legece done
aue sens paseir

ar chu la lar
gece done sene
tre ki est lons

ar chu asser om
les un coens don clo
stre sens plonc es sens
liuel

ar chu partom
one pire que les un
moities sont dretes

ar chu tor rom
le uis don persour

ar chu fait om
li uassas que si on
tient li tans que li am

Totes ces figures sunt
estrattes de geometrie.

ar chu tail om uosure riuleje

PLATE 56 GEOMETRICAL DEVICES II
(MASONRY) (C.XL)

The labels read from left to right, as follows:

Top row: How to make regular pendants: place upside down; How to obtain the diameter of a round object by placing it in a corner; How to gauge a right angle and how to make the keystone of a tierce-point arch (captions reversed); How to make the keystone of a fifth-point arch; Archimedes' spiral.

Middle row: How to join a four-cornered pillar; How to cut a voussoir by echelons; By this method is the spire of a church raised and its mold cut.

Bottom row: How to cut the voussoirs of hanging arches; How to set up two pillars of the same height without plumb line or level; How to measure the height of a tower.

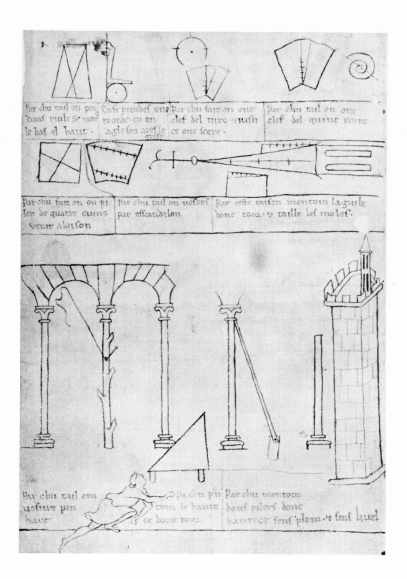

| Par chu tail on peſ dans mules · mar le bas el haut. | Enſi prندeſ one roonde en on a gleſ en arele groſ | Par chu fait on one clef del tire ruth ce one ſcere · | Par chu tail on one clef del quint point |

| Par chu fait on ou piller de quatre ouins venir aloiſon | Par chu tail on uoſouſ par eſcandelon | Par ceſte raison montom laguile donc roor · y taille leſ moleſ. |

| Par chu tail oma uoſiure pen haut · | Par chu pin roms le haute iſ ce donc roor. | Par chu montom douſ pilerſ donc hautece ſenſ plom · y ſenſ huel |

PLATE *57*   GEOMETRICAL DEVICES III
(MASONRY)   (C.XLI)

The labels read from left to right, as follows:

Top row: How to connect eight capitals with a single one, without crowding; this is an example of good masonry; How to place an egg beneath a pear so that, by taking the proper measures, the pear may fall on the egg.

Middle row: How to trace a five-cornered tower; How to find the center of a cut voussoir; How to round out a voussoir without a mold.

Bottom row: How to bevel the springing-stones gauged for each member without a mold; How to cut a cusped voussoir; How to make three kinds of arches with a single opening of the compass.

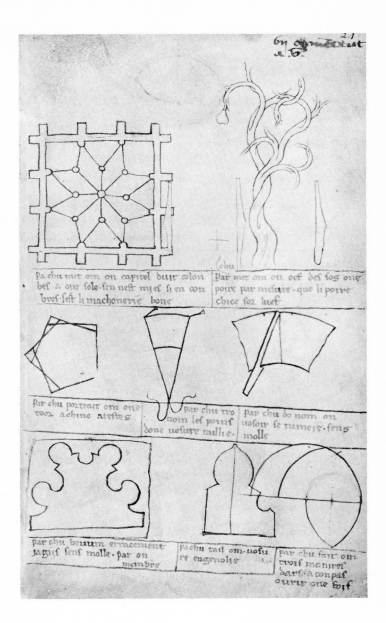

Pa chu met om on capitel dist colon
bel a one sole feu nest mies si en con
brel selt li machonerie bone

Par met om on oef del sos one
poire par mesure que li poire
chice sor hes

Par chu portrait om one
toor achine arestes

par chu tro
uom les poins
done uostre tailli e

par chu do nom on
uosour se rimese sens
molle

par chu bouum erracement
iagus sens molle par on
membre

pachu tail om uosu
re engenolie

par chu fait om
trois maniere
bars a conpas
ourir one fois

PLATE 58   GEOMETRICAL DEVICES IV
(MASONRY)   (C.XXXIV)

The labels read from left to right, as follows:

Top row: Here you may see the right kind of roof to place
over a vaulted chapel; And if you wish to see a
good and easily-made wooden roof, study this
one.

Bottom row: Here is a trussing for a strong penthouse; Here
is a sconce for monks to carry lighted; It can be
made to turn if you know how.

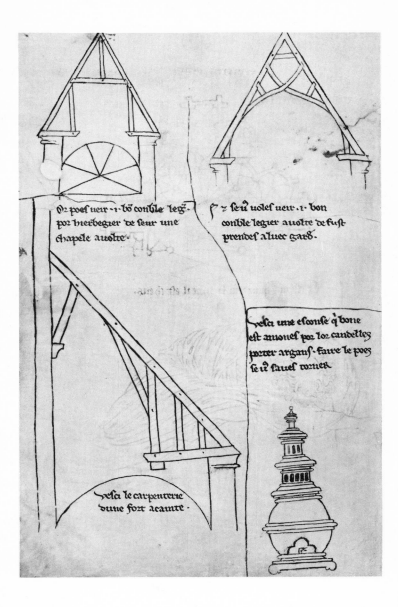

Or poes uern · i · bo conble legZ
por herbegier de seur une
chapele auostre·

Se u uoles uern · i · bon
conble legier auostre de fust
prendes aluec garB·

Veseu une esconse qͥ bone
est amones por lor candelleZ
porter arganſ· faire le poeZ
se uͥ sauef torner·

Vesci le carpenterie
dune fort acainte·

PLATE 59   GEOMETRICAL DEVICES V
         (ENGINES)   (C.XLIV)

The labels read from left to right, as follows:

Top row: How to make a saw operate itself; How to make
              a crossbow which never misses.

Middle row: How to make an angel keep pointing his finger
              toward the sun; How to make the most powerful
              engine for lifting weights.

Bottom row: How to make the eagle face the Deacon while
              the Gospel is being read.

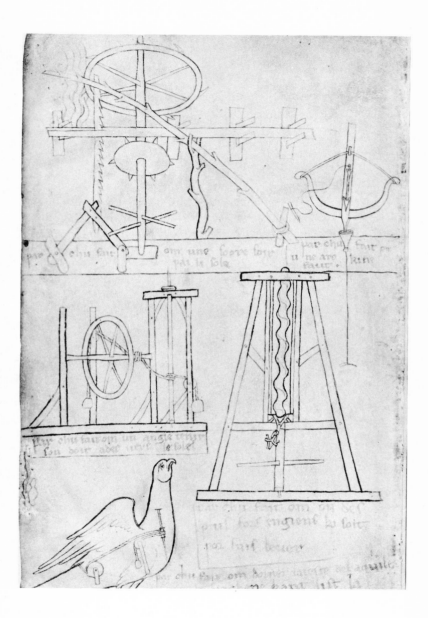

Par ce chu fait on une fort forte
fait le fole

par ce chu fait on
u ne arc kint

par chu fawon un angle tenent
son desir aber ueut a lolet

par chu fait on one sel
par del engient le loit
por darl louer

par chu fais on sonel autre of aquile

PLATE 60 GEOMETRICAL DEVICES VI
(ENGINES) (c.xlv)

The labels read from left to right, as follows:

Top row: By this means, one can cut off the tops of piles under water so as to set a pier on them; How to brace the spokes of a wheel without cutting the shaft.

Bottom row: How to straighten up a sagging house by using this kind of strut; How to work on a house or tower even if the timbers are too short.

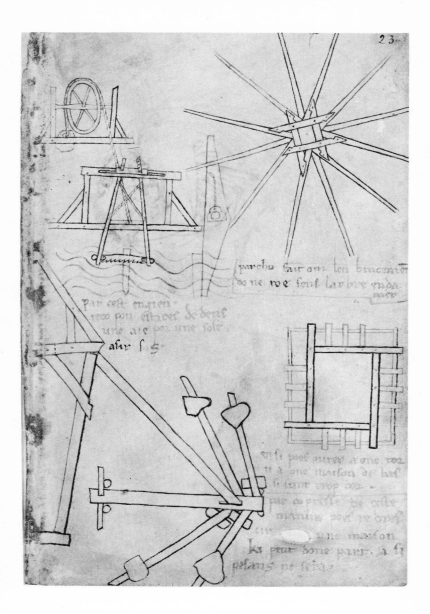

parchu fait om len binicmen
co ne roe fent larbre enda
paen

pur cest engien
reco pou estacer de dens
une ate pur une sole
asir s s.

orsi poet ourer a one roe
il a one maison de bas
si tant trop ceo.
par co puisse be ceste
maniue voe re one
cie une maison
les peut done purr. si fi
pesans ne selau.

PLATE 61   A CATAPULT   (c.lix)

The legend below reads: *If you wish to build that strong engine called the catapult, pay close attention. Here is the base as it rests on the ground. In front are the two windlasses and the double rope by which the pole is hauled down, as you may see on the other page. The weight which must be hauled back is very great, for the counterpoise is very heavy being a hopper full of earth. This is fully two fathoms long, eight feet wide, and twelve feet deep. Remember that before the bolt is discharged, it must rest on the front stanchion.*

(The page on which the other part of the engine is illustrated is missing.)

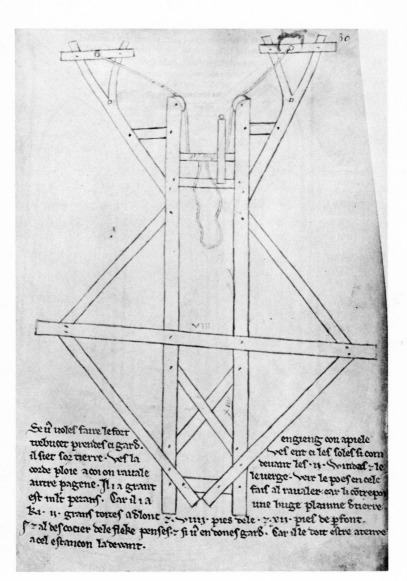

Se tu voles faire le fort
trebucet prendes ci gard.
il sier sor tierre. Ves la
corde ploie a coi on rauale
autre pagene. Il i a grant
est mlt pzans. Car il i a
ki · ij · grans toires a dlont · z · viij · pies dele · z · xij · pies de pfont.
sz · al descocier dele fleke penses z · si tu en dones gard. Car il te doit estre atenve
a cel estancon la devant.

engiens con apiele
Ves ent ci les soles si com
devant les · ij · Gundas z le
le verge. Ver le pos en cele
fars al raualer car li cotrepo
une huge plaine d'tierre.
z · viij · pies dele · z · xij · pies de pfont.

PLATE 62   A PERPETUAL MOTION MACHINE
(C.IX)

The legend below reads: *Often have experts striven to make a wheel turn of its own accord. Here is a way to do it with an uneven number of mallets and with quicksilver.* (To which a later hand has added: *I say Amen.*)

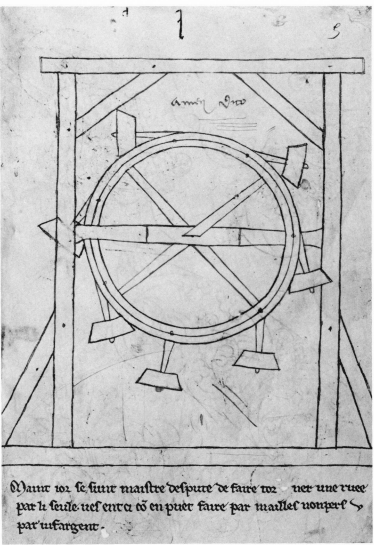

amen Dɲo

Maint tor se fuit maistre despute de faire tor   net une ruee
par li seule nef en ci tō eu puet faire par mailles nonpert ᛫
par nisargent᛫

PLATE 63 TWO UNFINISHED SKETCHES
(c.v)

Top of crucifix and Ionian capital.

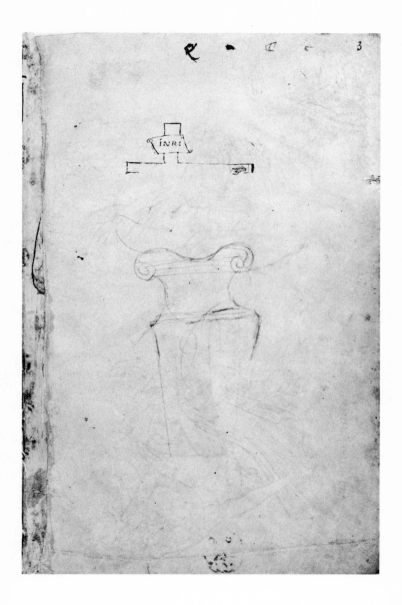

The caption above the wheel reads: *Here below are the figures of the Wheel of Fortune, all seven of them correctly pictured.*

Under the Wheel of Fortune, two recipes are given: one for ceramic paste, and the other for a depilatory. Their translation has been omitted.

ues la · ij · testes de fuelles ·

yesa desos les figures de le ruee
fortune · totes les · vij · j magenes

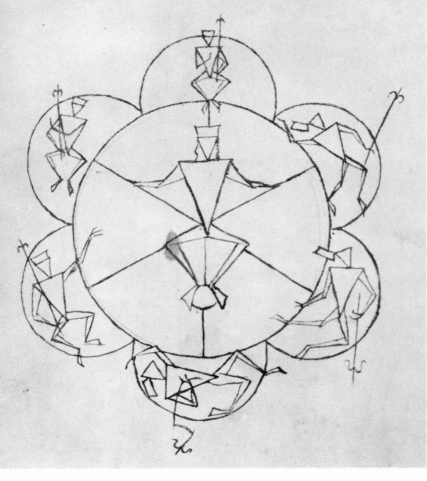

TABLE OF
CONCORDANCE

THE Roman numerals refer to the plates as they occur in the
Sketchbook today and in all standard editions.

1	I	22	LI	43	LX
2	II	23	XXII	44	LXIII
3	XXII	24	LVIII	45	LXII
4	XXI	25	XLIII	46	XX
5	VIII	26	X	47	LXIV
6	LV	27	XI	48	XXIX
7	LVI	28	XVII	49	XXX
8	XXVI	29	LII	50	XXXI
9	IV	30	LIII	51	XII
10	XV	31	XLVII	52	XIII
11	XXIII	32	XLVIII	53	LVII
12	XXIV	33	VII	54	LIV
13	VI	34	XIV	55	XXXIX
14	XLIX	35	XXXV	56	XL
15	XXV	36	XXXVI	57	XLI
16	XXVII	37	XXXVII	58	XXXIV
17	XXVIII	38	XXXVIII	59	XLIV
18	XLVI	39	XVIII	60	XLV
19	XVI	40	XIX	61	LIX
20	III	41	XXVIII	62	IX
21	L	42	LXI	63	V
				64	XLII

INDEX OF
SUBJECTS

(Reference is by plate number)